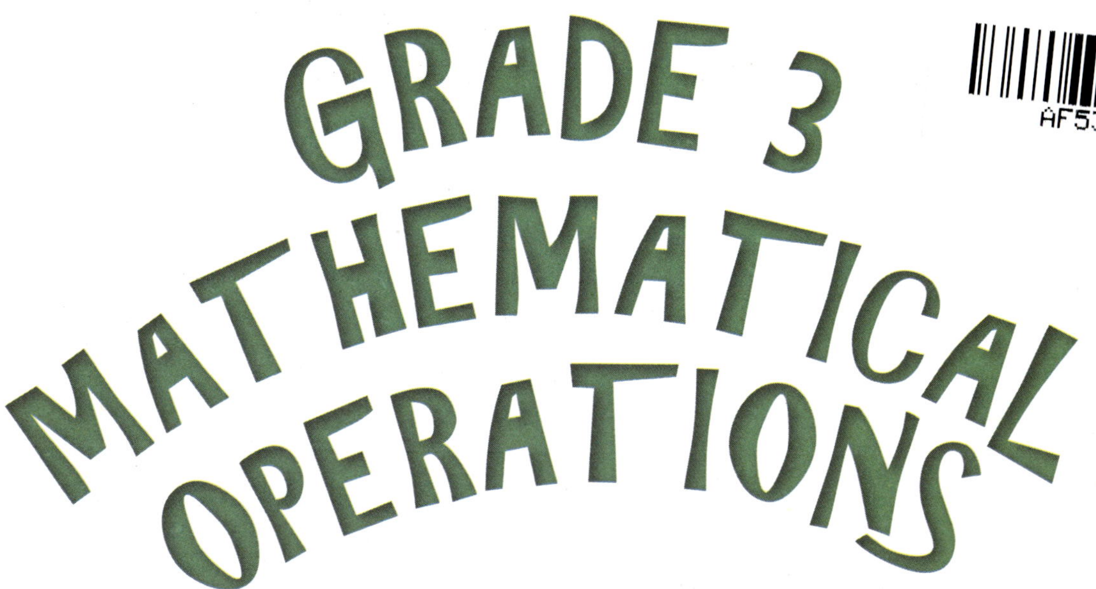

Fun-filled Activities

An imprint of Om Books International

ADDITION - 4 DIGIT NUMBERS WITHOUT REGROUPING

$$\begin{array}{r} 1554 \\ +\,2305 \\ \hline 3859 \end{array}$$

Step 1: Add the ones
Step 2: Add the tens
Step 3: Add the hundreds
Step 4: Add the thousands

IT IS TRUE!
Always arrange numbers according to their place value

$$\times \begin{array}{r} 298 \\ +\,45 \\ \hline \end{array} \qquad \checkmark \begin{array}{r} 298 \\ +\,45 \\ \hline \end{array}$$

Find the sum of the following.

$$\begin{array}{r} 7574 \\ +\,1123 \\ \hline \end{array} \quad \begin{array}{r} 4153 \\ +\,5746 \\ \hline \end{array} \quad \begin{array}{r} 2543 \\ +\,7453 \\ \hline \end{array} \quad \begin{array}{r} 2381 \\ +\,1111 \\ \hline \end{array}$$

$$\begin{array}{r} 3415 \\ +\,3423 \\ \hline \end{array} \quad \begin{array}{r} 2221 \\ +\,7167 \\ \hline \end{array} \quad \begin{array}{r} 4378 \\ +\,4411 \\ \hline \end{array} \quad \begin{array}{r} 1273 \\ +\,1212 \\ \hline \end{array}$$

$$\begin{array}{r} 3517 \\ +\,1321 \\ \hline \end{array} \quad \begin{array}{r} 2263 \\ +\,5723 \\ \hline \end{array} \quad \begin{array}{r} 4385 \\ +\,5414 \\ \hline \end{array} \quad \begin{array}{r} 5217 \\ +\,1132 \\ \hline \end{array}$$

$$\begin{array}{r} 4278 \\ +\,6011 \\ \hline \end{array} \quad \begin{array}{r} 4221 \\ +\,1231 \\ \hline \end{array} \quad \begin{array}{r} 8527 \\ +\,4431 \\ \hline \end{array} \quad \begin{array}{r} 8047 \\ +\,1710 \\ \hline \end{array}$$

$$\begin{array}{r} 1520 \\ +\,4479 \\ \hline \end{array} \quad \begin{array}{r} 3461 \\ +\,3325 \\ \hline \end{array}$$

$$\begin{array}{r} 1654 \\ +\,2035 \\ \hline \end{array} \quad \begin{array}{r} 7442 \\ +\,9313 \\ \hline \end{array}$$

$$\begin{array}{r} 5996 \\ +\,1002 \\ \hline \end{array} \quad \begin{array}{r} 7207 \\ +\,2231 \\ \hline \end{array}$$

Challenge

Which is the largest of all the answers on this page? Write it here and add 1001 to it. Write the sum.

ADDITION – 4 DIGIT NUMBERS WITH REGROUPING

Add

$$\begin{array}{r} 3965 \\ +\,4387 \\ \hline \\ \hline \end{array}$$

1. Add the ones and regroup.
   5 + 7 = 12 ones = 1 ten + 2 ones.
   Write 2 at the ones place and
   carry over 1 ten to the tens column
2. Add the tens.
   1 + 6 + 8 = 15 tens = 1 hundred and 5 tens
   Write 5 at the tens place and carry over
   1 hundred to the hundreds column.
3. Add the hundreds.
   1 + 9 + 3 = 13 hundreds= 1 thousands and 3 hundreds
   Write 3 at the hundreds place
   and carry over 1 thousand to the thousands column.
4. Add the thousands.
   1 + 3+4= 8
   The sum is 8352.

$$\begin{array}{r} {}^{1} \\ 3965 \\ +\,4387 \\ \hline 2 \\ \hline \end{array}$$

$$\begin{array}{r} {}^{1\,1} \\ 3965 \\ +\,4387 \\ \hline 52 \\ \hline \end{array}$$

$$\begin{array}{r} {}^{1\,1\,1} \\ 3965 \\ +\,4387 \\ \hline 352 \\ \hline \end{array}$$

$$\begin{array}{r} {}^{1\,1\,1} \\ 3965 \\ +\,4387 \\ \hline 8352 \\ \hline \end{array}$$

Add. Regroup as needed.

$$\begin{array}{r} 4278 \\ +\,6013 \\ \hline \\ \hline \end{array} \quad \begin{array}{r} 6540 \\ +\,7144 \\ \hline \\ \hline \end{array} \quad \begin{array}{r} 8527 \\ +\,4431 \\ \hline \\ \hline \end{array} \quad \begin{array}{r} 2381 \\ +\,8647 \\ \hline \\ \hline \end{array}$$

$$\begin{array}{r} 1528 \\ +\,1989 \\ \hline \\ \hline \end{array} \quad \begin{array}{r} 3465 \\ +\,8756 \\ \hline \\ \hline \end{array} \quad \begin{array}{r} 5996 \\ +\,1632 \\ \hline \\ \hline \end{array} \quad \begin{array}{r} 7207 \\ +\,2234 \\ \hline \\ \hline \end{array}$$

$$\begin{array}{r} 1654 \\ +\,2675 \\ \hline \\ \hline \end{array} \quad \begin{array}{r} 7442 \\ +\,9319 \\ \hline \\ \hline \end{array} \quad \begin{array}{r} 6982 \\ +\,7517 \\ \hline \\ \hline \end{array} \quad \begin{array}{r} 9739 \\ +\,1980 \\ \hline \\ \hline \end{array}$$

TICKLE YOUR BRAIN!

Fill in the boxes on the steps by solving the problems in the across and down box.

ACROSS

A. 5310 + 4543
B. 285 + 157
C. 364 + 367
D. 185 + 729
E. 8317 +1329
F. 4062 + 4733
G. 245 + 423
H. 517 + 177
I. 64 + 23

DOWN

J. 29 + 25
K. 221 + 126
L. 248 + 91
M. 72 + 47
N. 25 + 21
O. 31 + 17
P. 38 + 29
Q. 48 + 48
R. 289 + 277
S. 537 + 361
T. 17 + 30

ADDITION WORD PROBLEMS

Read and solve the word problems. Regroup where needed.

1. There were 2152 cans of food in the shelter pantry. 5104 more were packed. How many cans of food were there in all?

2. There were 6200 people at the amusement park. 2294 more came in. How many people were there in all?

3. There were 4301 fish at the aquarium. 2123 more were added. How many fish were there in all?

4. The painters had 3401 paint rollers to start. After they bought 1239 more, how many paint rollers did they have in all?

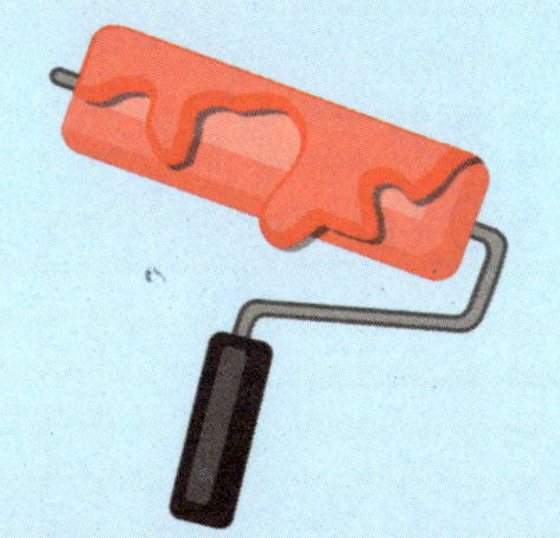

5. There were 1232 vehicles in the parking lot last week. 2567 more drove in this week. How many vehicles were there in all?

1. **Subtract** the **ones**

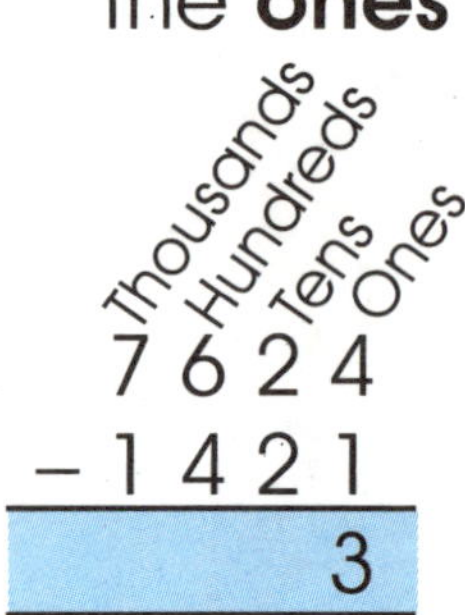

2. **Subtract** the **tens**

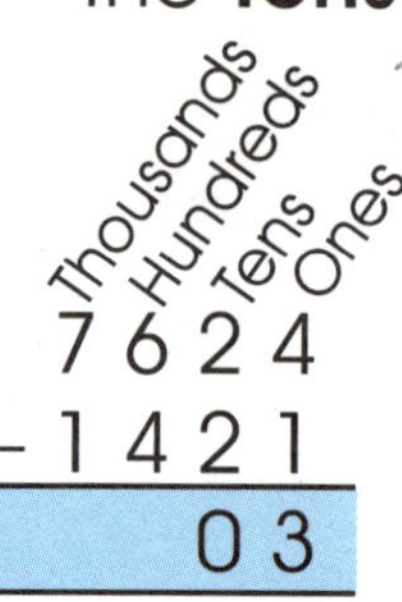

3. **Subtract** the **hundreds**

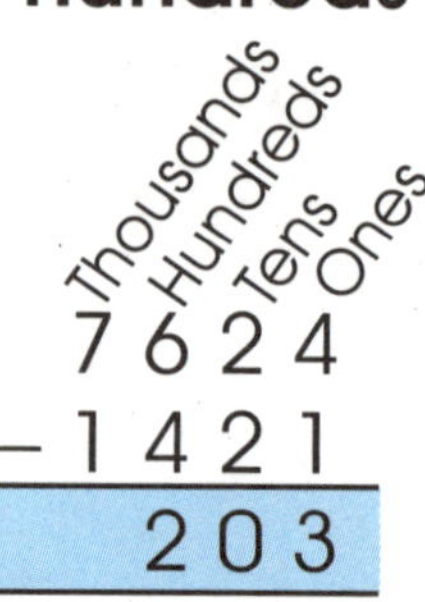

4. **Subtract** the **thousands**

Thousands	Hundreds	Tens	Ones
7	6	2	4
− 1	4	2	1
6	2	0	3

Subtract without regrouping.

7676 − 6364 ______	9558 − 6422 ______	7789 − 5336 ______	5588 − 1132 ______
8578 − 2254 ______	5989 − 1713 ______	6689 − 2144 ______	7878 − 6223 ______
8888 - 3246 ______	7758 − 2214 ______	7669 − 1233 ______	8859 − 3516 ______
8885 − 6000 ______	3868 − 2227 ______	8559 − 5049 ______	8498 − 7111 ______
7867 − 1143 ______	6292 − 3272 ______	7626 − 1001 ______	8734 − 4224 ______
2665 − 1022 ______	6297 − 2064 ______	3465 − 2223 ______	2531 − 1410 ______

SUBTRACTING 4-DIGIT NUMBERS WITH REGROUPING

Subtract

$$\begin{array}{r} 7086 \\ -3592 \\ \hline \\ \hline \end{array}$$

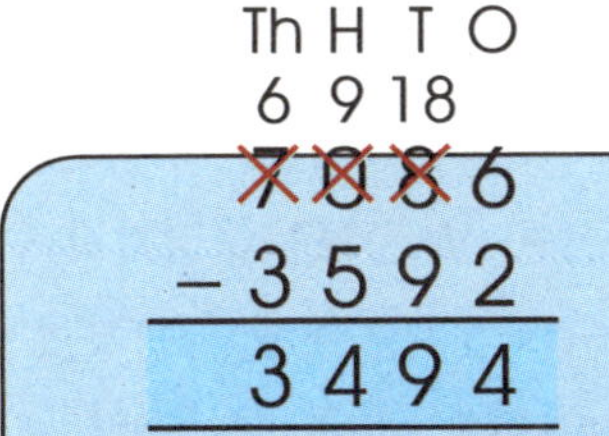

1. Subtract the ones first.
   6 – 2 can be done.
   6 – 2 = 4 ones
2. Subtract the tens.
   8 – 9 cannot be done
   Regroup 7 thousands, 0 hundreds, 8 tens as 6 thousands, 9 hundreds and 18 tens
   Now, 18 – 9 = 9 tens
3. Then subtract the hundreds.
   9 – 5 = 4 hundreds
4. At last subtract the thousands.
   6 – 3 = 3 thousands

IT IS TRUE!

The change in order of numbers cannot be followed in subtraction. The larger number should be on the top in a vertical subtraction problem.

Subtract by regrouping.

$$\begin{array}{r} 3515 \\ -2392 \\ \hline \\ \hline \end{array} \qquad \begin{array}{r} 6241 \\ -4599 \\ \hline \\ \hline \end{array} \qquad \begin{array}{r} 2561 \\ -1658 \\ \hline \\ \hline \end{array} \qquad \begin{array}{r} 9405 \\ -6286 \\ \hline \\ \hline \end{array}$$

$$\begin{array}{r} 9118 \\ -8592 \\ \hline \\ \hline \end{array} \qquad \begin{array}{r} 9078 \\ -6737 \\ \hline \\ \hline \end{array} \qquad \begin{array}{r} 6897 \\ -3003 \\ \hline \\ \hline \end{array} \qquad \begin{array}{r} 8069 \\ -7127 \\ \hline \\ \hline \end{array}$$

$$\begin{array}{r} 4840 \\ -1801 \\ \hline \\ \hline \end{array} \qquad \begin{array}{r} 6678 \\ -6367 \\ \hline \\ \hline \end{array} \qquad \begin{array}{r} 5274 \\ -5029 \\ \hline \\ \hline \end{array} \qquad \begin{array}{r} 8223 \\ -1814 \\ \hline \\ \hline \end{array}$$

$$\begin{array}{r} 3515 \\ -2392 \\ \hline \\ \hline \end{array} \qquad \begin{array}{r} 6241 \\ -4599 \\ \hline \\ \hline \end{array} \qquad \begin{array}{r} 2561 \\ -1658 \\ \hline \\ \hline \end{array} \qquad \begin{array}{r} 9405 \\ -6286 \\ \hline \\ \hline \end{array}$$

SUBTRACTION WORD PROBLEMS

Read the problems and solve them. Regroup if needed.

1. There were 4244 flowers in the flower shop. After 3126 of them were sold, how many flowers were left in the flower shop?

2. The school cafeteria had 1491 hot dogs to start. They served 768 of them. How many hot dogs are left in the school cafeteria?

3. There were 3610 kids at the carnival. After 1448 of them went away, how many kids were left at the carnival?

4. There were 3315 students in the school. After 1135 of them graduated, how many students were left in the school?

5. The city farm had 3670 pears to pack. They packed 2113 of them. How many pears are left to be packed?

PUZZLE TIME!

Start anywhere and collect five numbers by following the paths. Don't jump or go back over a path twice. What is the highest total you can make?

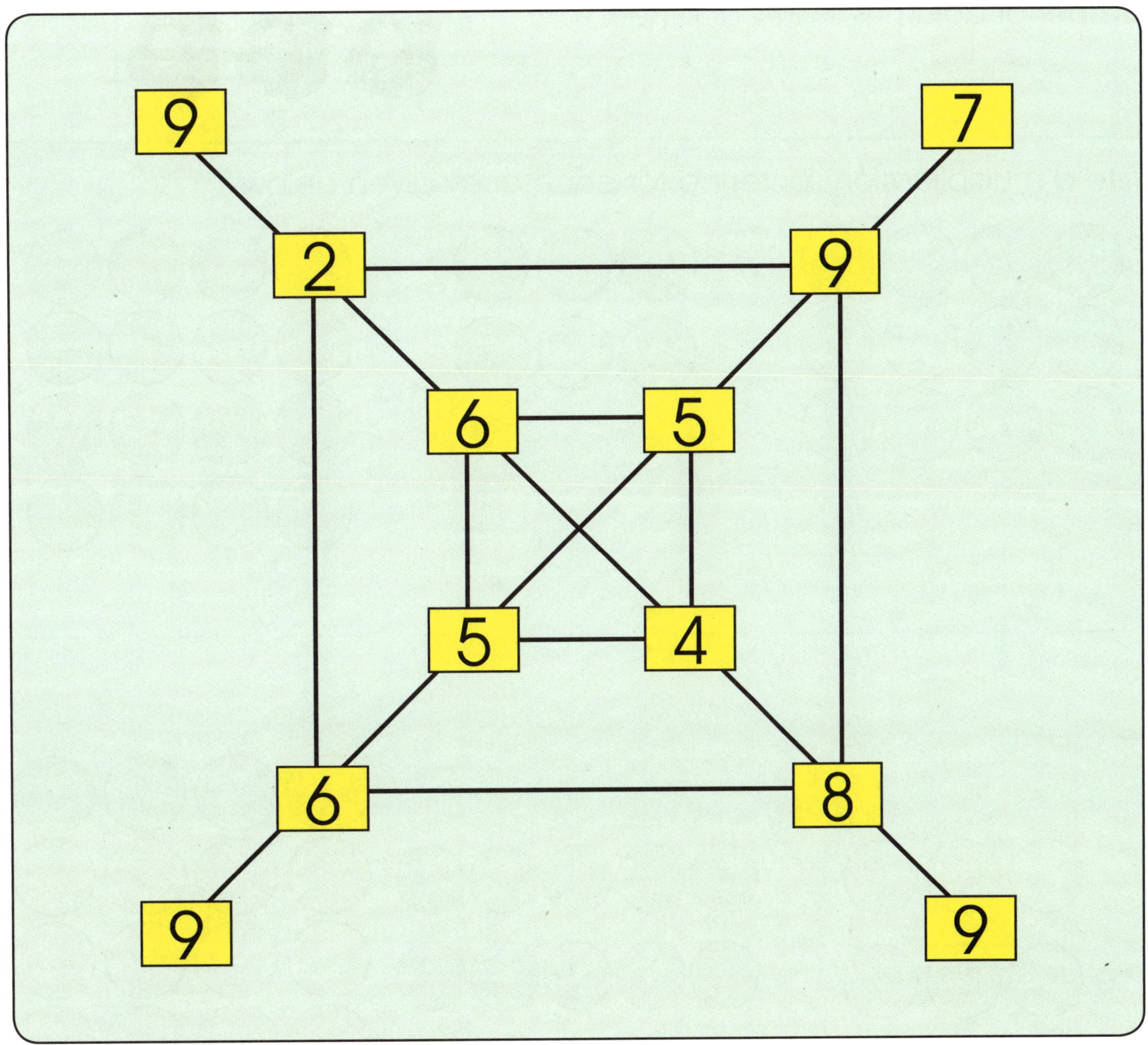

Challenge

Subtract your highest total with the lowest total you make. What's the answer?

ARRAYS

An array is an arrangement of rows and columns. We use an array to multiply numbers. The number of rows shows one factor and the number of columns shows another.

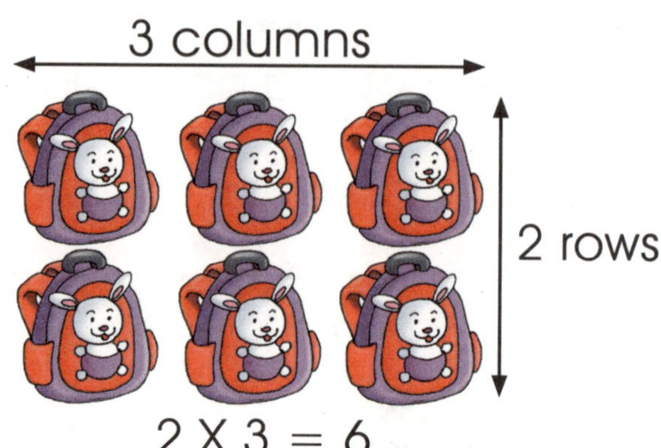

Write a multiplication sentence for each array given below.

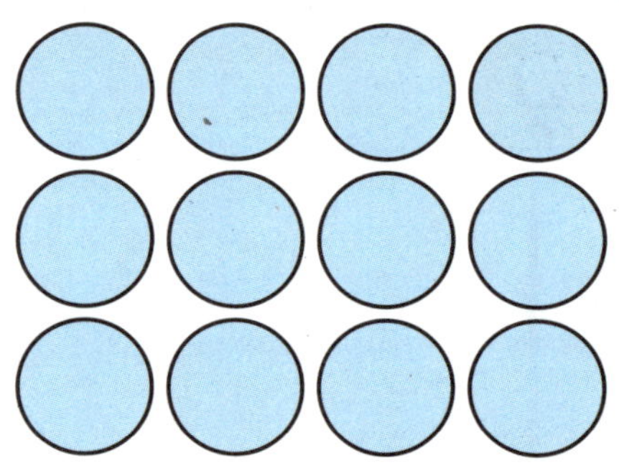

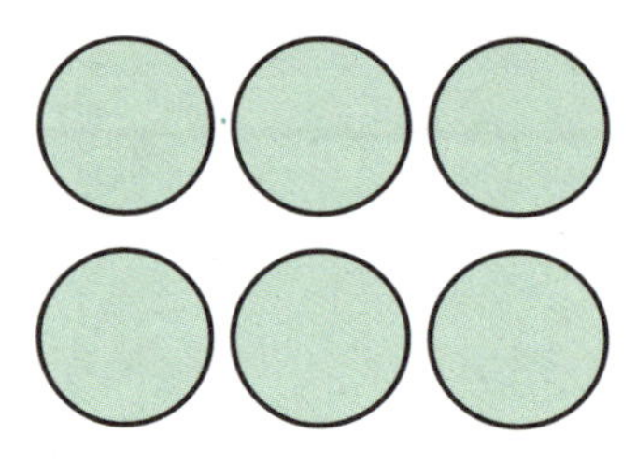

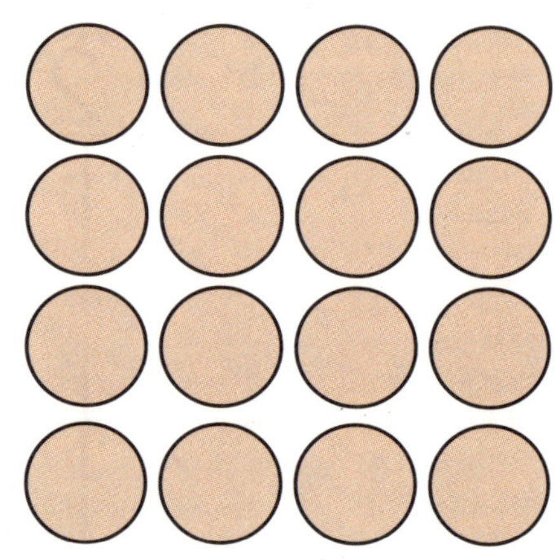

____ X ____ = ____   ____ X ____ = ____   ____ X ____ = ____

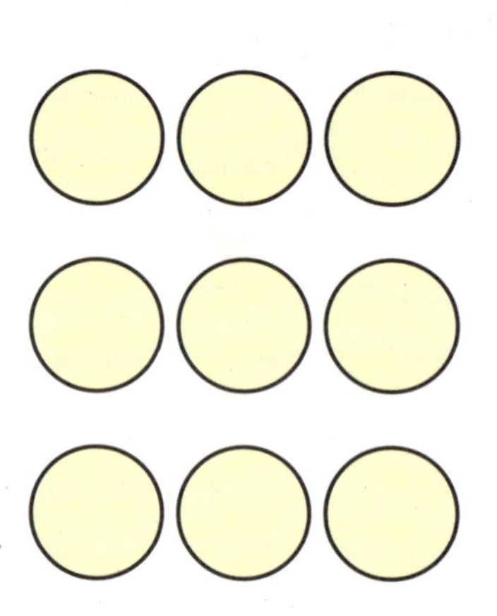

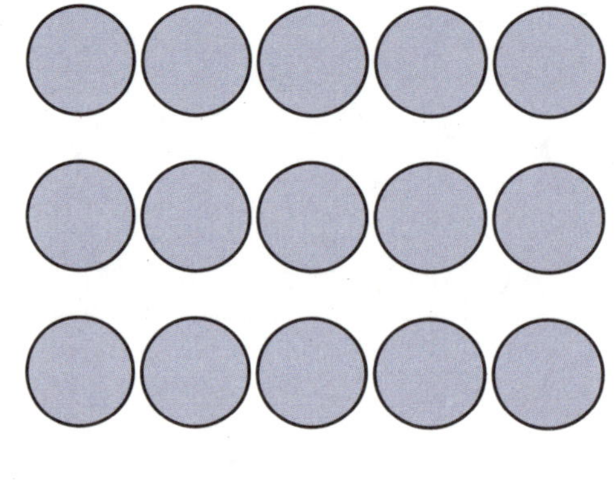

____ X ____ = ____   ____ X ____ = ____   ____ X ____ = ____

DISPLAYING ARRAYS

We draw objects in rows and columns to show arrays.

For example:

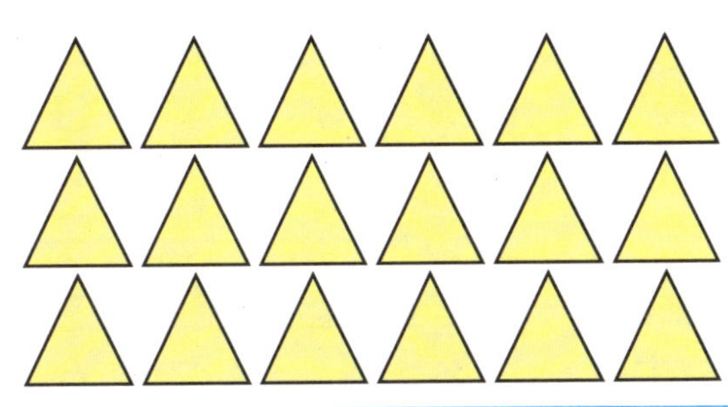

3 rows of 6

3 X 6 = 18

IT IS TRUE!

You can count all the objects in an array to check your answer.

Draw an array to show each multiplication sentence. Then write the answer.

1. 4 X 4 = __________

2. 5 X 2 = __________

3. 7 X 3 = __________

4. 2 X 6 = __________

5. 5 X 8 = __________

6. 9 X 4 = __________

Challenge

Draw two arrays that have the same product.

MULTIPLICATION TABLE

We use a multiplication table to learn number facts and find products.

In the table given alongside, we can see:

2 X 3 = 6

In the multiplication statement, 2 and 3 are factors and 6 is the product.

X	0	1	2	3	4	5	6
0	0	0	0	0	0	0	0
1	0	1	2	3	4	5	6
2	0	2	4	6	8	10	12
3	0	3	6	9	12	15	18
4	0	4	8	12	16	20	24
5	0	5	10	15	20	25	30

How to fill the table?

1. Multiply the number in the "ROW" by the number in the "COLUMN."
2. Then place the answer in the correct box.

Use the above table to find the product.

1. 3 X 3 = ________
2. 4 X 2 = ________
3. 5 X 4 = ________
4. 3 X 6 = ________
5. 2 X 5 = ________
6. 4 X 6 = ________
7. 5 X 5 = ________
8. 2 X 6 = ________
9. 5 X 3 = ________
10. 3 X 4 = ________

Challenge

Write your own multiplication statements using the table on this page.

MULTIPLICATION TABLE

Complete the multiplication table.

x	0	1	2	3	4	5	6	7	8	9	10
0											
1								14			
2											
3											
4											
5							30				
6			12								
7											
8											
9						45					
10											100

Write true or false for these multiplication statements. Use the table to verify your answer.

1. 2 X 9 = 68 ________
2. 7 X 8 = 56 ________
3. 7 X 4 = 28 ________
4. 9 X 4 = 36 ________
5. 6 X 6 = 45 ________
6. 8 X 8 = 79 ________
7. 8 X 3 = 24 ________
8. 5 X 9 = 45 ________

MULTIPLICATION FACTS

Now when you know your multiplication tables, it's easy to write multiplication facts.

We write multiplication facts to show two factors that have the same product.

24

3x8 4x6

IT IS TRUE!

A pair of facts like 4 X 6 is the same as 6 X 4 because it has the same factors.

Write all multiplication facts that have the following products.

56 ________________	36 ________________
48 ________________	18 ________________
40 ________________	32 ________________
64 ________________	20 ________________
20 ________________	35 ________________
42 ________________	50 ________________

40

2X20

4X10

5X8

8X5

FAST FACTS!

Time yourself and write these facts in just 3 minutes. Get, set, go!

a. 6 x 9 =_______ b. 3 x 9 =_______ c. 6 x 3 =_______

d. 3 x 7 =_______ e. 6 x 7 =_______ f. 2 x 7 =_______

g. 7 x 2 =_______ h. 7 x 7 =_______ i. 3 x 9 =_______

j. 2 x 8 =_______ k. 3 x 4 =_______ l. 2 x 5 =_______

m. 3 x 5 =_______ n. 6 x 6 =_______ o. 8 x 2 =_______

p. 4 x 6 =_______ q. 9 x 5 =_______ r. 6 x 8 =_______

s. 9 x 6 =_______ t. 5 x 7 =_______ u. 7 x 8 =_______

How many facts could you write in 3 minutes?

FIND THE MISSING FACTOR

$$\begin{array}{r} 6 \\ \times\ \boxed{?} \\ \hline 48 \end{array}$$

6 times what number equals to 48?

$$\begin{array}{r} 6 \\ \times\ \boxed{8} \\ \hline 48 \end{array}$$

Complete each multiplication sum by writing the missing number.

$\begin{array}{r} 5 \\ \times 3 \\ \hline \_\_ \end{array}$	$\begin{array}{r} 7 \\ \times 6 \\ \hline \_\_ \end{array}$	$\begin{array}{r} \square \\ \times 3 \\ \hline 18 \end{array}$	$\begin{array}{r} 2 \\ \times 4 \\ \hline \_\_ \end{array}$	$\begin{array}{r} \square \\ \times 1 \\ \hline 1 \end{array}$
$\begin{array}{r} 9 \\ \times \square \\ \hline 27 \end{array}$	$\begin{array}{r} 6 \\ \times 10 \\ \hline \_\_ \end{array}$	$\begin{array}{r} 8 \\ \times \square \\ \hline 40 \end{array}$	$\begin{array}{r} 4 \\ \times 6 \\ \hline \_\_ \end{array}$	$\begin{array}{r} 7 \\ \times \square \\ \hline 28 \end{array}$
$\begin{array}{r} 10 \\ \times 4 \\ \hline \_\_ \end{array}$	$\begin{array}{r} 7 \\ \times \square \\ \hline 63 \end{array}$	$\begin{array}{r} 3 \\ \times \square \\ \hline 6 \end{array}$	$\begin{array}{r} \square \\ \times 10 \\ \hline 80 \end{array}$	$\begin{array}{r} 8 \\ \times 3 \\ \hline \_\_ \end{array}$

11 TIMES AND 12 TIMES TABLE

Look across and down the number grid to complete the 11 and 12 times multiplication table.

11	2	22	56	43	11	4	44
34	66	33	55	22	77	91	32
11	56	11	88	99	44	22	11
6	34	5	22	34	56	13	3
66	33	55	44	67	11	89	33
55	77	88	99	00	7	11	99
11	8	88	65	67	77	89	65
67	54	34	11	9	99	79	00

12	1	12	35	24	76	54	23
23	54	34	12	66	12	3	36
56	48	12	6	65	4	89	76
34	67	2	72	45	48	78	99
64	12	24	24	55	73	18	19
12	5	60	45	12	7	84	90
8	62	74	24	78	90	34	28
96	38	65	12	9	108	88	99

MULTIPLYING TWO-DIGIT NUMBERS WITHOUT REGROUPING

Multiply the ones.

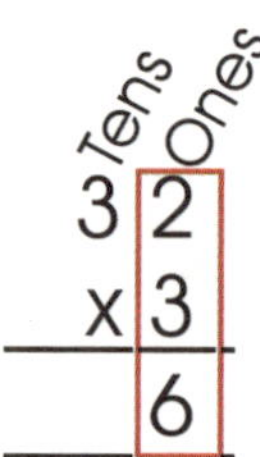

Multiply the tens.

Tens
Ones

3	2
x	3
9	6

Multiply and write the product.

32 x 2 = ____	13 x 3 = ____	23 x 3 = ____	11 x 5 = ____	22 x 4 = ____
12 x 3 = ____	22 x 4 = ____	10 x 5 = ____	11 x 9 = ____	10 x 9 = ____
11 x 8 = ____	12 x 4 = ____	13 x 2 = ____	23 x 2 = ____	99 x 1 = ____
22 x 2 = ____	34 x 2 = ____	41 x 2 = ____	44 x 2 = ____	10 x 8 = ____

MULTIPLYING TWO-DIGIT NUMBERS WITH REGROUPING

1. Multiply the ones and regroup.
2. Multiply the tens.
3. Then add the regrouped ones.

7 ones X 3 ones = 21
Regroup as 2 tens and 1 one

```
  27
 x 3
 ---
   1
```

3 ones X 2 tens = 6 tens
6 tens + 2 tens = 8 tens

```
   2
  27
 x 3
 ---
  81
```

Multiply

88 x 5	55 x 7	22 x 7	91 x 2
57 x 7	18 x 3	50 x 2	21 x 7
48 x 6	41 x 9	37 x 4	47 x 3

MULTIPLICATION WORD PROBLEMS

Solve each problem.

1. There were 3 buses. Each bus had 63 students. What was the total number of students?

2. Tim gave 5 stickers each to 36 of his friends. How many stickers did he give away?

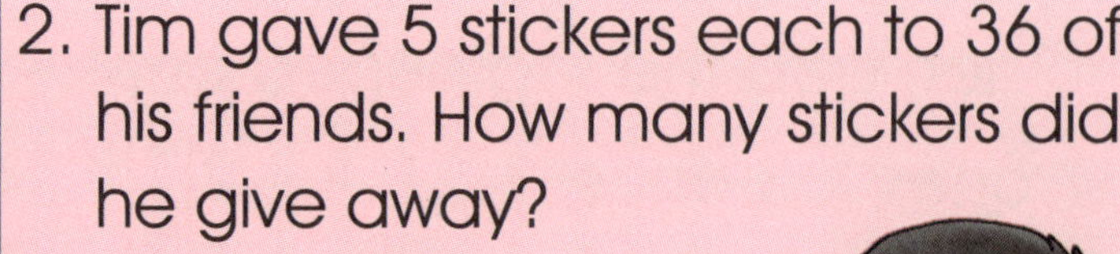

3. Mary sang 3 songs in each performance. There were 7 performances. How many times did Mary sing?

4. Christine bought 6 boxes of erasers. Each box had 42 erasers. How many erasers does Christine have?

5. There were 12 roses in each bouquet at the flower shop. If there were 4 bouquets, how many roses are there in all?

6. Max bought 6 bags of jellybeans. If each bag has 24 jellybeans, what is the total amount that he has?

Challenge

How many fingers are there in 20 hands? Write your answer in 3 seconds without multiplying!

DIVISION

Division is making equal groups or splitting into equal parts.

8 divided into 2 groups
= 4 in each group.

$8 \div 2 = 4$

8 divided into 4 groups
= 2 in each group

$8 \div 4 = 2$

Write division statements for the pictures given below.

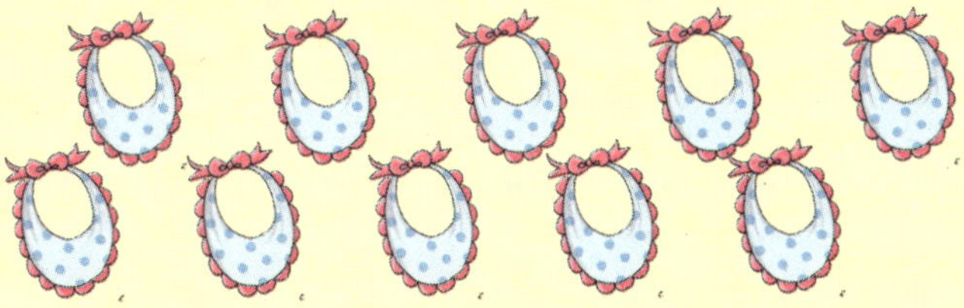

DIVISION BY 2 AND 3

There are 2 groups of cats.
Each group has 6 cats.

$12 \div 2 = 6$

Here there are 3 groups.
Each group has 4 cats.

$12 \div 3 = 4$

Draw a circle around the group of fish to show the division fact.

$16 \div 2 =$ ________

$27 \div 3 =$ ________

Solve these division facts.

a. $18 \div 2 =$ ____________

b. $10 \div 2 =$ ____________

c. $14 \div 2 =$ ____________

d. $8 \div 2 =$ ____________

e. $6 \div 2 =$ ____________

f. $20 \div 2 =$ ____________

g. $15 \div 3 =$ ____________

h. $21 \div 3 =$ ____________

i. $12 \div 3 =$ ____________

j. $24 \div 3 =$ ____________

k. $9 \div 3 =$ ____________

l. $18 \div 3 =$ ____________

DIVISION BY 4 AND 5

Circle the balls to show the division fact.

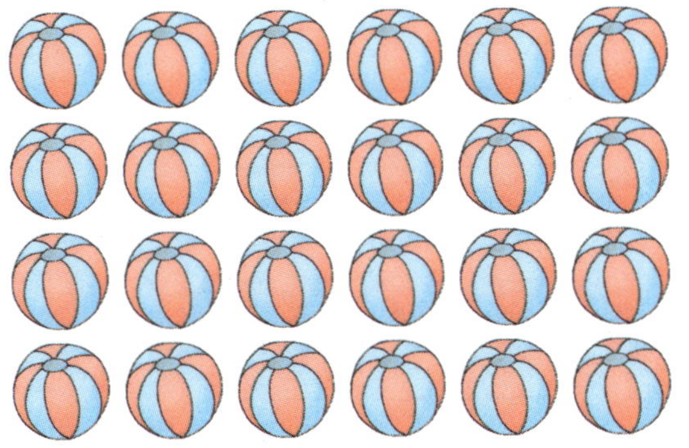

24 ÷ 4 = ________

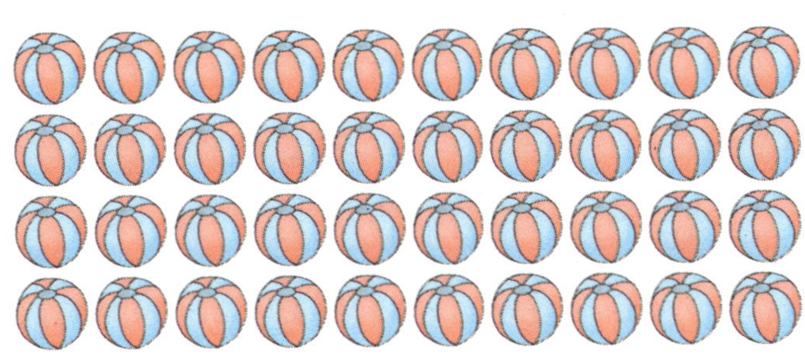

40 ÷ 5 = ________

Solve these division facts.

a. 24 ÷ 4 = ___________

b. 20 ÷ 4 = ___________

c. 8 ÷ 4 = ___________

d. 12 ÷ 4 = ___________

e. 28 ÷ 4 = ___________

f. 16 ÷ 4 = ___________

g. 32 ÷ 4 = ___________

h. 40 ÷ 4 = ___________

i. 36 ÷ 4 = ___________

j. 15 ÷ 5 = ___________

k. 20 ÷ 5 = ___________

l. 5 ÷ 5 = ___________

m. 30 ÷ 5 = ___________

n. 35 ÷ 5 = ___________

o. 10 ÷ 5 = ___________

p. 25 ÷ 5 = ___________

q. 40 ÷ 5 = ___________

r. 45 ÷ 5 = ___________

QUICK TIP!

Division is the opposite of multiplication. If you know your tables well, you can solve, write division facts.

DIVISION BY 6 AND 7

Practice these division facts.

a. 6 ÷ 6 = ____________

b. 12 ÷ 6 = ____________

c. 18 ÷ 6 = ____________

d. 24 ÷ 6 = ____________

e. 30 ÷ 6 = ____________

f. 36 ÷ 6 = ____________

g. 42 ÷ 6 = ____________

h. 48 ÷ 6 = ____________

i. 54 ÷ 6 = ____________

j. 60 ÷ 6 = ____________

k. 7 ÷ 7 = ____________

l. 14 ÷ 7 = ____________

i. 21 ÷ 7 = ____________

n. 28 ÷ 7 = ____________

o. 35 ÷ 7 = ____________

p. 42 ÷ 7 = ____________

q. 49 ÷ 7 = ____________

r. 56 ÷ 7 = ____________

s. 63 ÷ 7 = ____________

t. 70 ÷ 7 = ____________

Fill in the missing numbers to complete the division facts.

a. ☐ ÷ 7 = 5

b. 63 ÷ ☐ = 9

c. 49 ÷ ☐ = 7

d. ☐ ÷ 7 = 6

e. 70 ÷ ☐ = 10

f. ☐ ÷ 7 = 3

g. 84 ÷ ☐ = 12

h. 77 ÷ ☐ = 11

i. ☐ ÷ 7 = 8

j. 42 ÷ ☐ = 7

Challenge

Write 3 division facts that have number 20 as answer.

DIVISION BY 8 AND 9

Practice these division facts.

a. 9 ÷ 9 = ____________

h. 24 ÷ 8 = ____________

b. 56 ÷ 8 = ____________

i. 9 ÷ 9 = ____________

c. 72 ÷ 8 = ____________

j. 56 ÷ 7 = ____________

d. 40 ÷ 4 = ____________

k. 90 ÷ 9 = ____________

e. 36 ÷ 9 = ____________

l. 16 ÷ 8 = ____________

f. 40 ÷ 8 = ____________

m. 81 ÷ 9 = ____________

g. 27 ÷ 9 = ____________

n. 8 ÷ 8 = ____________

FACT FAMILY- DIVISION AND MULTIPLICATION

A fact family is a group of math facts that uses the same numbers.

6 X 4 = 24   4 X 6 = 24

24 ÷ 4 = 6   24 ÷ 6 = 4

Write a fact family for each group of numbers.

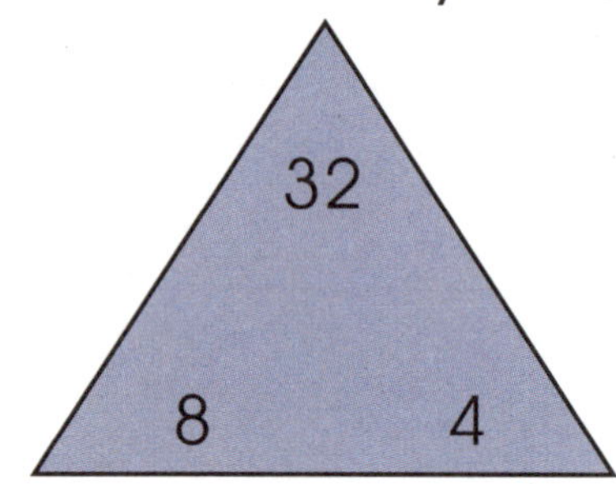

_____ X _____ = _____

_____ X _____ = _____

_____ ÷ _____ = _____

_____ ÷ _____ = _____

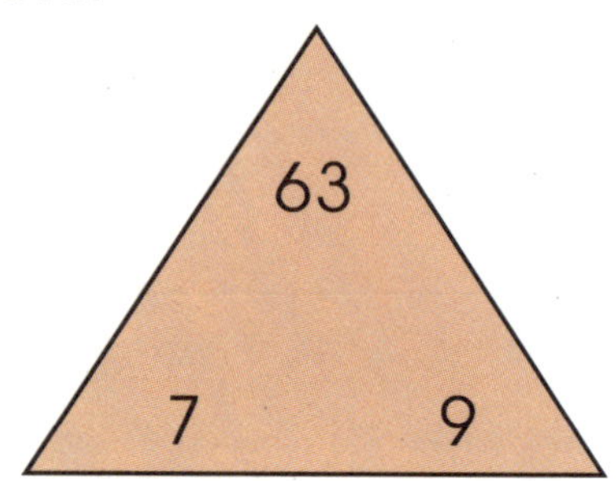

_____ X _____ = _____

_____ X _____ = _____

_____ ÷ _____ = _____

_____ ÷ _____ = _____

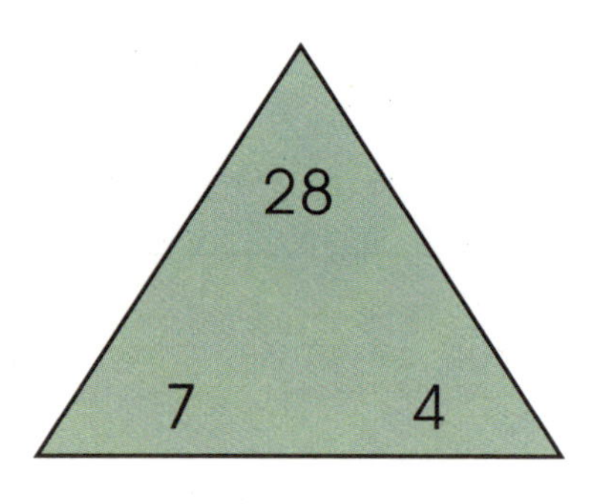

_____ X _____ = _____

_____ X _____ = _____

_____ ÷ _____ = _____

_____ ÷ _____ = _____

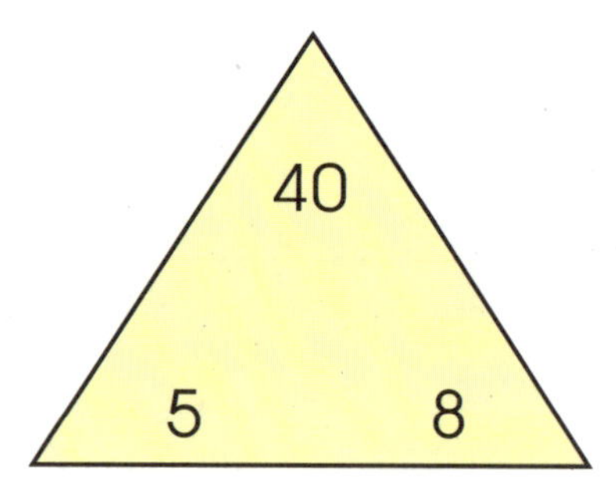

_____ X _____ = _____

_____ X _____ = _____

_____ ÷ _____ = _____

_____ ÷ _____ = _____

DIVISION WORD PROBLEMS

Solve each problem.

1. Mary, Nancy, and Tom have 24 erasers all together. If the erasers are equally divided, how many will each person get?

____

2. Joan has 48 green balloons. She wants to give her four friends the same number of green balloons, how many will each friend get ?

____

3. Mary goes fishing with Tim. They catch 16 trout. If they equally split up the trout, how many will each one get ?

____

4. Mary was at the beach for five days and found 32 seashells. She plans to give all of her seashells equally to her eight friends. How many seashells will each friend get ?

____

5. There were a total of 27 hockey games during the three month season. If the games are equally divided, how many hockey games were played in each month ?

____

TICKLE YOUR BRAIN

Fill in the blanks of the crossword with the correct numbers to make the division sentences correct.

64	÷		=	8			÷	2	=	27
÷				÷		÷				÷
	÷		=	2			÷	2	=	
=				=		=				=
32			÷		=	9				9

				36	÷		=2	23		68
÷				÷		÷				÷
12			÷		=					
=				=		=				=
12	÷		=	4			÷	1	=	

YOUR TURN!

Make your own division puzzle. Each figure in the picture below is a hexagon. A hexagon has 6 sides. Write a division or multiplication statement in each hexagon that gives the answer 6.
How many statements could you make?

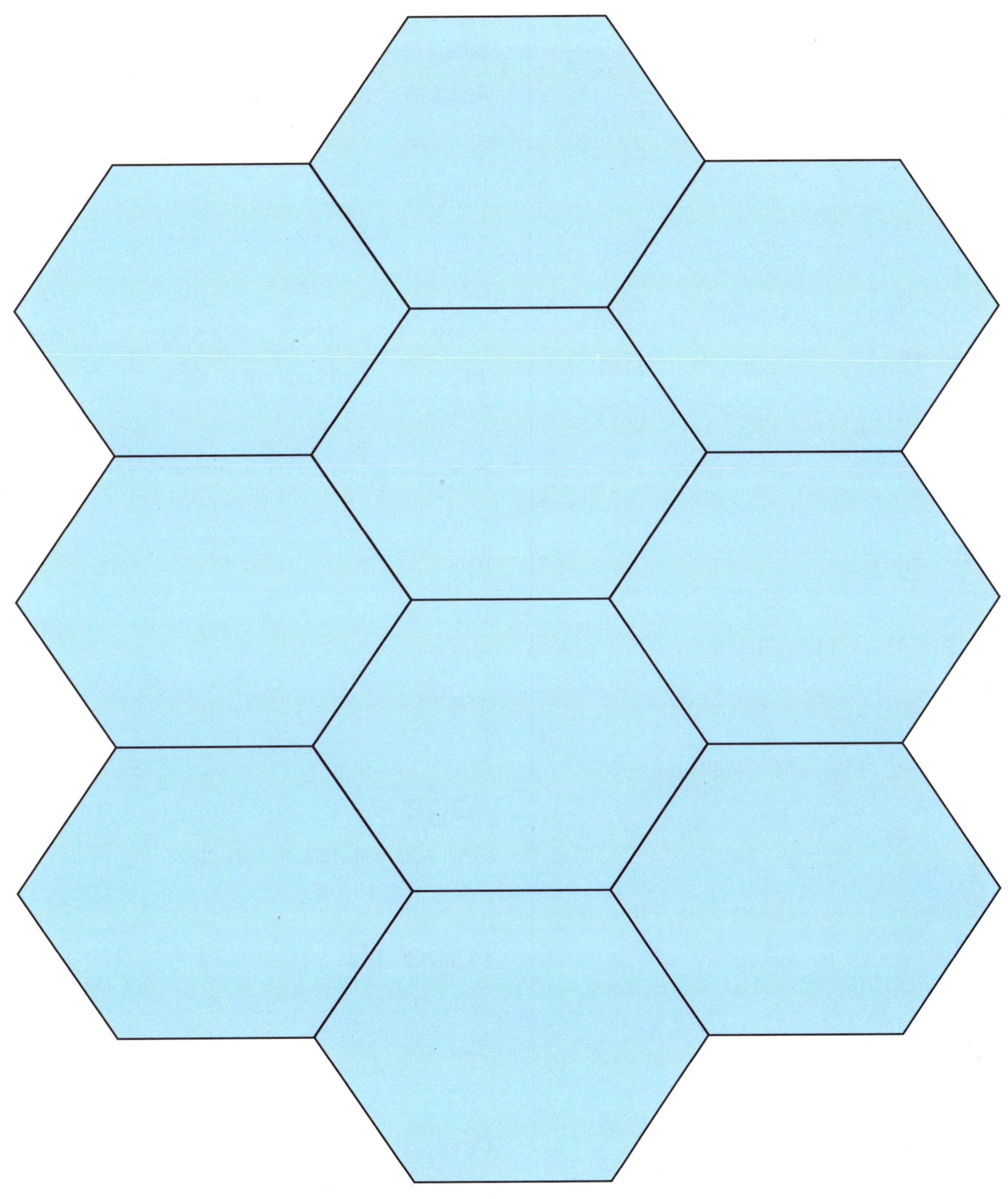

ANSWER KEY

Page 2

1. 8697	7. 9899	13. 9996	20. 3492
2. 6838	8. 9388	15. 8789	21. 2485
3. 4838	9. 7986	16. 9799	22. 6349
4. 10289	10. 5452	17. 12958	23. 9757
5. 5999	11. 6786	18. 6998	24. 9438
6 3689	12. 16755	19. 13999	25. 10739

Page 3

10291	13684	12958	11028
3517	12221	7628	9441
4329	16761	14499	11719

Page 4

Across

9853 442 731 914 9646 8795 668
694 87

Down

54 347 339 119 46 48 67 96
566 898 47

Page 5

7256

8494

6424

4640

3799

Page 6

1312	3136	2453	4456
6324	4276	4545	1655
5642	5544	6436	5343
2885	1641	3510	1387
6724	3020	625	4510
1643	4233	1242	1121

Page 7

1123	1642	903	3119
526	2341	3894	942
3039	311	556	6409
1123	1642	903	3119

Page 8

1118

723

2162

2180

1557

Page 9

Children will do on their own

Page 10

3x4 =12	2X3 =6	4X4 =16
3X3 =9	3X5 =15	5X4 =20

Page 11

Children will do on their own.

Page 12

9	24
8	25
20	12
18	15
10	12

Page 13

Children will do on their own.

Statements that are true and false:

1. False
2. True
3. True
4. True
5. False
6. False
7. True
8. True

Page 14

Since the students are aware of tables till 10, the facts are from tables 2-12

56 – 7 x8, 8x7

36 – 4x9, 9x4, 12x3, 3x12

48 – 6x8, 8x6, 12x4, 4x12

18 – 2x9, 9x2, 3x6, 6x3

40 – 5x8, 8x5, 4x10, 10x4

32 – 4x8, 8x4

64 – 8x8

20 – 2x10, 4x5, 5x4, 10x2

35 – 5x7, 7x5

42 – 6x7, 7x6

50 – 5x10, 10x5

Page 15

54	27	18
21	42	14
14	49	27
16	12	10
15	36	16
24	45	48
54	35	56

Page 16

15	42	3	8	1
3	60	5	24	4
40	9	2	8	24

Page 17

Children will do on their own

Page 18

64	39	69	55
88			
36	88	50	99
90			
88	48	26	46
99			
44	68	82	88
80			

Page 19

440	385	154	182
399	54	100	147
288	369	148	141

Page20

189	180
21	252
48	144

Page 21

9 ÷ 3 = 3	10 ÷ 2 = 5	10 ÷ 5 = 2
8 ÷ 2 = 4	8 ÷ 4 = 2	16 ÷ 8= 2
16 ÷ 8= 2	20 ÷ 4 = 5	20 ÷ 5 = 4
10 ÷ 2 = 5	10 ÷ 5 = 2	

Page 22

children will draw circle on their own.

16 ÷ 8= 2

27 ÷ 3= 9

a. 9	b. 5	c. 7
d. 4	e. 3	f. 10
g. 5	h. 7	i. 4
j. 8	k. 3	l. 6

Page 23

children will draw circle on their own.

24 ÷ 4= 6

40 ÷ 5= 8

8	3
5	4
2	1
3	6
7	7
4	2
8	5
10	8
9	9

Page 24

a. 1	b. 2	c. 3	d. 4
e. 5	f. 6	g. 7	h. 8
i. 9	j. 10	k. 1	l. 2
m. 3	n. 4	o. 5	p. 6
q. 7	r. 8	s. 9	t. 10

a. 35	b. 7	c. 7	d. 42
e. 7	f. 21	g. 7	h. 7
i. 56	j. 6		

Page 25

a. 1	b. 7	c. 9	d. 7
e. 4	f. 5	g. 3	h. 3
i. 1	j. 8	k. 10	l. 2
m. 9	n. 1		

Page 26

Children will do on their own

Page 27

1. 8	2. 12
3. 8	4. 4
5. 9	

Page 28

Children will do on their own

Page 29

Children will do on their own